Highlights™

Hidden Pictures®

Splish Splash

Super Challenge Puzzles

HIGHLIGHTS PRESS
Honesdale, Pennsylvania

Welcome, Hidden Pictures® Puzzlers!

When you finish a puzzle, check it off √. Good luck, and happy puzzling!

Contents

Cover art by Mark Corcoran

On the Beach

crown, nail, open book, lollipop, snake, pencil, toothbrush, slice of pie, ladder, ice-cream cone, crescent moon, mug

Art by R. Michael Palan

Sand Castle

flip-flop, bird, slice of cake, wishbone, star, surfboard, flag, hat, swim fin, sailboat, shovel, 

Art by Maurie Jo Manning

Low Tide

bell, pushpin, mug, slice of pie, toothbrush, carrot, spoon, slice of bread, needle, safety pin, mitten, cupcake

Art by Charles Jordan

Mega Challenge!
Find 15 Hidden Objects!

Shore Fun

Art by Chauncy

A Flurry of Flamingoes

pliers, elf's hat, fish, ice pop, pencil, rabbit, needle, apple, hammer, shoe, screwdriver, horn

Art by Leslie Franz

Kite-Flying Contest

party hat, slice of pizza, toothbrush, snail, baseball bat, 2 rings, slice of cake, pine tree, bell, pencil, crown, necktie, fan, porcupine, bowl, fish

Art by Diana Zourelias

Beach Turtles

boot, toothbrush, fishhook, clown's hat, sock, slipper, pencil, spoon, paper clip, plunger, pear, nail, ice-cream cone, iron, teakettle

Art by Valeri Gorbachev

Shore Games

penguin, banana, seal, hammer, paintbrush, rabbit, tack, nail, crayon, ring, flag

Art by Maurie Jo Manning

Fun in the Sun

closed book, paper clip, needle, iron, trumpet, fishhook, mouse, squirrel, caterpillar, bird, shoe, glove, straight pin, strawberry, pennant, turtle, telephone receiver, ice-cream cone, roller skate, car, shoe,

clothespin, mitten, bell, fork, penguin, ladle, duck, ant

Art by Valeri Gorbachev

Goin' Fishing

muffin, lollipop, ice-cream cone, coffeepot, butter knife, bat, feather, turtle, needle, crescent moon, rabbit, umbrella, duck, apple, mouse

Art by Bill Colrus

Hawaiian Hibernation

Mega Challenge!
Find 15 Hidden Objects!

Art by Tim Davis

Octopus Plays the Sax

floatie, arrow, mouse, fork, bird, dragonfly, spoon, snail, key, fishhook, tack, paper clip, coat hanger, toothbrush

Art by Valeri Gorbachev

Angelfish Pair

three-leaf clover, dog bone, light bulb, shuttlecock, mermaid, seal, lizard, butter knife, button, apple, turtle, bird, rattlesnake

Art by Scott Edwin Carle

On Duty

hammer, whale, pencil, sock, slice of pie, boot, pine tree, bird, tennis racket, spoon, ice-cream cone, carrot, book, golf club

Art by R. Michael Palan

The Uninvited Guests

chick, paper clip, duck, bell, dog, mushroom, bowl, toothbrush, seal, elephant, lizard, penguin, sock, parrot

Art by Mij Colson-Barnum

Shuffleboard Game

sock, whale, spoon, mushroom, colander, ice pop, crown, teacup, feather, bell, worm, iron, ladder, pennant

Art by Diana Zourelias

Mega Challenge!
Find 12 Hidden Objects!

Surfside Fun

Art by George Wildman

Just Beachy

wishbone, high-heeled shoe, carrot, ruler, teacup, rabbit, crown, nail, fishhook, sock, toothbrush, mitten, pennant, cherry, spoon, fork, baseball bat, pencil, saltshaker, pointy hat

Art by Mike DeSantis

Surf Riders

slice of lemon, golf club, doughnut, toothbrush, banana, envelope, ruler, fishhook, dustpan, spoon, flag, slice of pie

Art by David Helton

Down the River

lollipop, glove, candle, sneaker, broom, funnel, teacup, frying pan, flashlight, banana, spoon, flag

Art by Rocky Fuller

What a Catch!

hat, worm, ring, golf club, crescent moon, needle, slipper, wishbone, carrot, artist's brush, apple, nail, fishhook, crayon, heart

Art by R. Michael Palan

Checkmate

pointy hat, high-heeled boot, bowling pin, duck, slice of pie, carrot, caterpillar, canoe, dragonfly, pencil, musical note, bird, toothbrush, ice skate, broom, cupcake, sailboat, fish

Art by Linda Weller

Mega Challenge!
Find 13 Hidden Objects!

Outrigger Outing

Art by Rocky Fuller

Triple Leapfrog

wishbone, closed umbrella, bell, paper clip, light bulb, heart, sailboat, dog, crescent moon, pencil, toothbrush, crown

Art by Tim Davis

Lighthouse Slide

pennant, coat hanger, handbell, oar, hockey stick, bat, pickax, domino, snake, golf club, kite, pencil, fishhook, spatula, heart

Art by Arieh Zeldich

At the Beach

slice of cake, bird, glove, caterpillar, fried egg, dinosaur, teacup, ice-cream bar, closed umbrella, cowboy hat, pencil, bell, bowl

Art by Susan T. Hall

Swan Lake

glove, canoe, ring, crescent moon, pennant, toothbrush, hat, heart, slice of pie, sock, screwdriver, paintbrush, funnel, lollipop, mug, needle, spoon, telescope, candle, muffin, bell, seal

Art by Linda Weller

Lakeside Beach

sailboat, nail, hockey stick, drinking straw, spider, pennant, musical note, flag, flashlight, eyeglasses, envelope, telephone receiver, tack, butter knife, carrot, teacup

Art by Chuck Dillon

Surprise Catch

needle, slice of pizza, nail, butterfly, mug, shovel, mallet, muffin, clothespin, sock, mitten, can

Art by George Wildman

Fore!

snake, glove, cane, banana, needle, slice of pie, mushroom, sock, pickax, teacup, tube of toothpaste, candle, hat, bow, artist's brush

Art by George Wildman

Teatime

spoon, hot dog, drum, toothbrush, sock, ladder, crescent moon, tack, closed umbrella, acorn, party hat

Art by Chris Forrest

First Swim

ballet slipper, carrot, bowl, banana, hot dog, ghost, necktie, canoe

Art by Paula Pertile

Setting Off

duck, wishbone, spatula, spoon, flashlight, fish, pear, needle, mug, slice of pie, apple core, slice of lemon

Art by Maurie Jo Manning

Family Hike

golf club, hammer, butterfly, boot, tack, candle, needle, toothbrush, carrot, tube of toothpaste, elf's hat, nail, slice of bread, seashell, banana

Art by R. Michael Palan

City Lake Park

fishhook, nail, mitten, bell, ladder, needle, hat, slipper, open book, slice of cake, ring, teacup, cupcake, key, lollipop, snake, hoe, spool of thread, fish, mallet, heart, trowel, candle, ice-cream cone, pitcher,

envelope, pennant, sailboat, ice-cream bar, funnel, shovel, slice of pie, flashlight, carrot

Art by Olivia Cole

Scuba Divers

butter knife, heart, crescent moon, sock, toothbrush, apple, pencil, fishhook, bell, paper clip, bird, boomerang, bowling pin, hat

Art by Debra Spina Dixon

Armchair Adventurer

Mega Challenge!
Find 16 Hidden Objects!

Art by Ellen Appleby

Beach Play

ladle, dog bone, snail, dinosaur, camel, teacup, the number 2, duck, sailboat, chick, bird, spade

Art by Jill Droppa

On the Boardwalk

sailboat, spade, telescope, bowl, needle, flowerpot, hockey stick, wrench, high-heeled shoe, spoon, crescent moon, necktie, mitten, pennant, ice-cream cone, arrow, musical note

Art by Lynn Adams

Beach Volleyball

ice-cream cone, nail, party hat, bell, banana, egg, light bulb, high-heeled boot, canoe, eyeglasses, toothbrush, teacup, pencil, duck, wishbone, comb

Art by Tim Davis

Emperor Angelfish

Mega Challenge!
Find 20 Hidden Objects!

Art by Joe Seidita

Sand Architects

spoon, shark, nail, pencil, slice of pizza, table-tennis paddle, fish, paintbrush, the letter E, ice-cream bar, carrot, duck

Art by R. Michael Palan

Hippo Takes a Snooze

candle, banana, mushroom, tack, funnel, flower, mallet, crayon, pen, slice of cake, ice-cream bar, key

Art by Charles Jordan

Whale Watching

heart, carrot, boot, bat, telephone receiver, ghost, egg, mug, slice of pizza, pencil, eyeglasses, banana, shovel

Art by Bill Colrus

Off to School

needle, light bulb, snake, heart, carrot, ring, ice-cream cone, envelope, ruler, saltshaker, comb, crown

Art by Liz Ball

Bottom Feeding

eyeglasses, pencil, dog bone, paper airplane, ring, tree, bowl, mouse, flag, banana, funnel, wishbone

Art by George Wildman

Sea Horse

sock, candy corn, swim fin, snake, mitten, artist's brush, canoe, comb, baseball cap, drinking glass, toothbrush, hatchet, trowel, flyswatter, caterpillar, sailboat, mushroom, spoon

Art by Joe Seidita

Kites Aloft

tack, purse, slice of watermelon, flashlight, coat hanger, arrow, open book, light bulb, mug, penguin, domino, sailboat, banana, crescent moon

Art by Maurie Jo Manning

Wind Surfing

Mega Challenge!
Find 14 Hidden Objects!

Art by Tim Davis

Bears at the Beach

spoon, pennant, saltshaker, fish, clothespin, toothbrush, sock, ice-cream bar, chicken drumstick, acorn, slice of pie, boot, candle, ring, teacup, spade

Art by R. Michael Palan

Beach Bunnies

pushpin, pencil, golf club, artist's brush, toothbrush, musical note, magnifying glass, safety pin, nail, fishhook, bell, teacup

Art by Charles Jordan

Playful Dolphins

nail, crescent moon, pencil, artist's brush, piece of popcorn, mitten, saucepan, golf club, teacup, swan, book, musical note

Art by R. Michael Palan

Sea Turtle World

vase, scrub brush, shuttlecock, slice of bread, saucepan, balloon, pear, baseball, pea pod, glove, bell, barbell

Art by George Wildman

Just Cruising

carrot, button, barbell, walnut, baseball, heart, vase, umbrella, jump rope, crescent moon, cap, baseball bat, doughnut

Art by George Wildman

Cats at the Beach

saltshaker, ice-cream bar, book, slice of pie, leaf, artist's brush, chicken drumstick, tack, horseshoe, musical note, carrot, snake, toothbrush

Art by R. Michael Palan

Playing with Hula-Hoops

pie, kite, carrot, slice of pizza, spoon, snake, horseshoe, bell, muffin, candy cane, magnet, lollipop, artist's brush, magnifying glass, sailboat, pennant, party hat, banana, teacup, crown, wedge of orange, belt, caterpillar, book

Art by Lyn Martin

Mega Challenge!
Find 16 Hidden Objects!

No Time for Lunch

Art by Mary Sullivan

Catch of the Day

fried egg, candle, sailboat, comb, pencil, wristwatch, envelope, olive, sock, needle, ice-cream cone, toothbrush

Art by Liz Ball

Marina Morning

shovel, flashlight, artist's brush, carrot, key, mitten, fishhook, feather, mallet, spatula, mushroom

Art by Charles Jordan

Mega Challenge!
Find 14 Hidden Objects!

Bears Go Fishing

Art by Valeri Gorbachev

Lunch Break

needle, slice of pizza, football, nail, screwdriver, bowl, artist's brush, snake, mallet, flag, ice-cream cone, mushroom

Art by George Wildman

The Beacon

paintbrush, open book, banana, slice of pizza, dog, mallet, pie, snake, funnel, spoon, hat

Art by George Wildman

Octopus on Guard

toothbrush, bell, mushroom, pushpin, sock, artist's brush, tack, hockey stick, pencil, ladle, teacup, spoon

Art by Charles Jordan

Boardwalk Visitors

ring, canoe, book, golf club, snake, sailboat, envelope, pencil, caterpillar, dustpan, toothbrush, ice-cream cone

Art by David Helton

A New Day

pencil, snake, baseball cap, game piece, butter knife, jump rope, funnel, spoon, candle, pom-pom, sock, fried egg, golf club

Art by George Wildman

Lighthouse Lookout

duck, slice of pie, teacup, candle, shoe, glove, heart, ice-cream cone, star, hammer, top hat

Art by R. Michael Palan

Mega Challenge!
Find 12 Hidden Objects!

Seal Watching

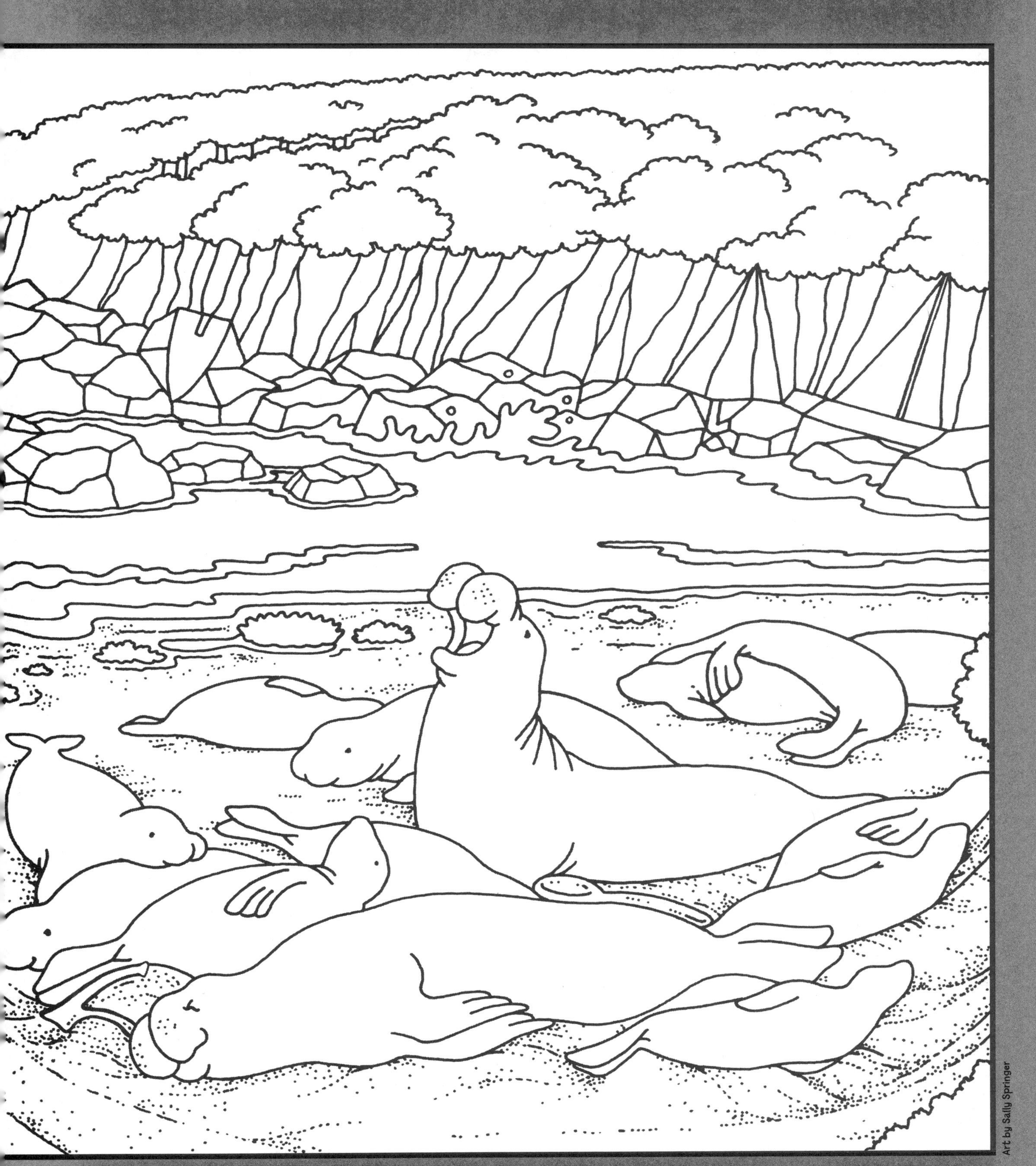

Art by Sally Springer

A Great Day for Sailing

open book, telescope, hat, spoon, crown, jump rope, oilcan, kite, needle, banana, whisk broom, mitten

Art by George Wildman

Castle Builders

teacup, ice-cream cone, cat, hatchet, pencil, thimble, seal, bird, mushroom, nail, saucepan, duck, leaf, artist's brush

Art by Leslie Franz

Crocs Ahoy!

needle, heart, open book, hatchet, banana, toothbrush, saw, comb, boot, ice-cream cone, pencil, bell, shoe

Art by Tim Davis

Painters' Paradise

bowling pin, candle, slice of pie, chef's hat, bottle, flowerpot, spider, paper airplane, watermelon, turtle, carrot

Art by George Wildman

A Friendly Wind

fried egg, ice-cream cone, pair of pants, crown, sock, toothbrush, artist's palette, pinwheel, ring, bowl, slice of pie, needle, football

Art by George Wildman

To the Lighthouse

Mega Challenge! Find 16 Hidden Objects!

Art by R. Michael Palan

Water World

baseball cap, candle, comb, artist's brush, hammer, drinking straw, clothespin, leaf, lollipop, ring, nail, toothbrush

Art by R. Michael Palan

Magic Castle

fish, artist's brush, spatula, slice of cake, musical note, funnel, leaf, pencil, fishhook, candle, eyeglasses, golf club, flowerpot, knitted hat

Art by Charles Jordan

Welcome Home

3 birds, bell, violin, 2 cats, key, sock, iron, 2 kangaroos, teacup, belt, rabbit

Art by Valeri Gorbachev

Wind-Surfing Monkeys

slice of watermelon, slice of pizza, slipper, flag, banana, doughnut, ring, leaf, flute, hat, boomerang, candy cane

Art by Marilee Harrald-Pilz

Under the Wild Cherry Tree

pennant, crescent moon, butterfly, flowerpot, cupcake, candle, teacup, sailboat, toothbrush, shoe, heart, mitten, funnel, lollipop, spoon, tulip, hammer, toucan, needle, paintbrush, ring

Art by Linda Weller

Stork's Landing

Mega Challenge!
Find 16 Hidden Objects!

STORK'S LANDING

Art by Arieh Zeldich

Ollie Octopus

flute, crown, ladle, toothbrush, pencil, arrow, mushroom, button

Art by Marilee Harrald-Pilz

Sailing Fun

musical note, shovel, ice-cream cone, fishhook, toothbrush, flag, crescent moon, pennant, heart, needle, slice of pizza, tack, pencil, question mark

Art by Sally Springer

Shell Collectors

bowl, toothbrush, crown, wishbone, slice of pizza, bell, mushroom, ice-cream cone, candle, arrow, boot, needle, flashlight

Art by Mary Sullivan

The Oceaneers

butterfly, plunger, crescent moon, can of paint, light bulb, wedge of cheese, ladle, toothbrush, anchor, caterpillar, teacup, tape dispenser, screwdriver, lemon, slice of watermelon, heart, oven mitt, spoon

Art by Rocky Fuller

Shower Power

artist's palette, lollipop, top hat, mushroom, egg, book, mallet, snake, ant, slice of pie, paper airplane, ring, nail

Art by George Wildman

Boating on the Bay

fishhook, banana, crown, toothbrush, golf club, boot, mallet, artist's brush, spoon, tack, pencil, pennant, needle

Art by R. Michael Palan

She Sells Seashells

slice of pie, canoe, pencil, lima bean, candle, cherries, ruler, paper airplane, banana, heart, clothespin, magnet, golf club, ice-cream cone

Art by Ron Lieser

Fishy Fun

Mega Challenge!
Find 13 Hidden Objects!

Art by Susan T. Hall

Ship Trip

envelope, dinner plate, glove, feather, pencil, ring, golf club, nail, bracelet, button, book, candle, sock, brick

Art by David Helton

Cowabunga!

snow cone, muffin, fried egg, ring, slice of pizza, slice of watermelon, mitten, banana, hat, spoon, carrot, pencil, crown

Art by Marilee Harrald-Pilz

Beach Day

Mega Challenge!
Find 23 Hidden Objects!

Art by Diana Zourelias

Pool Time Fun

yo-yo, rolling pin, needle, sock, hairbrush, party hat, fried egg, mitten, heart, wedge of orange, cactus, present, slice of pizza, cane, crayon

Art by Deborah Johnson

Cat Fish

chick, spool of thread, ghost, boot, bracelet, thimble, worm, light bulb, wrench, toothbrush, leaf, slipper

Art by Mary Sullivan

At the Seashore

glove, cupcake, banana, funnel, toothbrush, bell, baseball bat, pencil, mug, flying disk, safety pin, candle, chili pepper, slice of bread, crescent moon, spoon

Art by Maggie Swanson

Monkey Island

fish, tack, toothbrush, fishhook, hammer, golf club, crescent moon, ring, carrot, slice of cake, pine tree, needle, slipper, pitcher, mushroom

Art by R. Michael Palan

Four Friends at the Beach

saucepan, mallet, heart, flag, slice of pizza, snake, lollipop, button, fishhook, paper airplane, pennant, bowling ball, trowel, mug, banana, crown, nail, spatula, sock, ice-cream cone, ring

Art by Olivia Cole

Hit the Beach!

hamburger, wedge of orange, snake, boot, flag, mallet, toothbrush, acorn, worm, slice of pie, glove, banana, ring, pickax, pencil, flashlight, ice pop, Easter egg, hockey stick, pineapple, sailboat, can, spoon, rabbit, mushroom

Art by Chuck Dillon

Tall Ships on Parade

hand mirror, flying disk, coat hanger, golf club, heart, plunger, closed umbrella, needle and thread, hammer, light bulb, mug, mallet, fishhook, pennant, baseball bat, boomerang

Art by Arieh Zeldich

Catch a Wave

marshmallow, snake, golf club, kite, ring, slice of pie, cane, house, banana, feather, ladle, spatula

Art by David Helton

Piggy Water-Skiing Show

spoon, coffeepot, heart, banana, crown, golf club, teacup, mitten, sock, pencil, shoe, candle, button, wishbone, bat, musical note, artist's brush, crayon, crescent moon

Art by Mike DeSantis

Manatee Tea Party

Mega Challenge! Find 20 Hidden Objects!

Art by Mark Corcoran

Surfing School

ice-cream bar, nail, crescent moon, toothbrush, cane, question mark, needle, ice-cream cone, heart, bird, slice of pie, fishhook, hockey stick, artist's brush, slice of pizza, flag

Art by Sally Springer

Dinner with the Crabs

leaf, heart, paper clip, slipper, bracelet, pair of pants, banana, walnut, snake, chili pepper, binoculars, sock, tweezers, glove

Art by David Helton

Mega Challenge! Find 34 Hidden Objects!

Musical Fish

Art by René Mitchell-Mills

Beach Party

ghost, teapot, firefighter's helmet, artist's palette, high-heeled shoe, crown, feather, vase, flowerpot, comb, party hat, banana, hatchet, baseball bat, ice-cream cone, wedge of cheese, toy top, oilcan

Art by Mark Corcoran

Shell Castle

bird, eyeglasses, flip-flop, knitted hat, star, seashell, bottle, shovel, kite, fish, crown, crab

Art by Frank Bolle

A Day at the Beach

pennant, teacup, hockey stick, carrot, worm, kite, needle, button, crown, scissors, bowl, ice-cream cone, bell, saw, tack, ring, comb

Art by Lyn Martin

Fish and Chips

hockey stick, nail, ladder, coat hanger, football, mallet, key, bell, fishhook, plunger, ring, golf club, wedge of orange, fishhook, crescent moon, eyeglasses, hat pin

Art by Arieh Zeldich

Sand Art

artist's brush, ring, feather, teacup, spoon, flashlight, paintbrush, ladle, snake, golf club, pencil, ice-cream cone

Art by David Helton

Follow the Pilot

pickax, baseball bat, crescent moon, fork, seal, fishhook, flag, spool of thread, domino, ladder, button, hockey stick, comb, pen, shoe, magnet, coat hanger, nail

Art by Arieh Zeldich

▼Pages 4-5

▼Page 6

▼Page 7

▼Page 8

▼Page 9

▼Pages 10-11

▼Page 12

Answers

▼Page 13

▼Pages 14-15

▼Page 16

▼Page 17

▼Page 18

▼Page 19

▼Page 20

▼Page 21

Answers

▼Pages 22-23

▼Page 24

▼Page 25

▼Pages 26-27

▼Pages 28-29

▼Page 30

Answers

▼Page 31

▼Page 32

▼Page 33

▼Page 34

▼Page 35

▼Page 36

▼Page 37

▼Page 38

▼Page 39

Answers

▼Page 40

▼Page 41

▼Page 42

▼Page 43

▼Pages 44-45

▼Page 46

▼Page 47

▼Page 48

Answers

▼Page 49

▼Page 50

▼Page 51

▼Page 52

▼Page 53

▼Page 54

▼Page 55

▼Page 56

▼Page 57

Answers

▼Page 58

▼Page 59

▼Page 60

▼Page 61

▼Pages 62-63

▼Page 64

▼Page 65

▼Page 66

Answers

▼Page 67

▼Pages 68-69

▼Page 70

▼Page 71

▼Page 72

▼Page 73

▼Page 74

▼Page 75

Answers

▼Pages 76-77

▼Page 78

▼Page 79

▼Pages 80-81

▼Page 82

▼Page 83

▼Page 84

Answers

▼Page 85

▼Page 86

▼Page 87

▼Pages 88-89

▼Page 90

▼Page 91

▼Page 92

▼Page 93

▼Page 94

▼Page 95

▼Page 96

▼Page 97

▼Page 98

▼Page 99

▼Pages 100-101

▼Page 102

Answers

▼Page 103

▼Pages 104-105

▼Page 106

▼Page 107

▼Page 108

▼Page 109

▼Pages 110-111

Answers

▼Page 112

▼Page 113

▼Page 114

▼Page 115

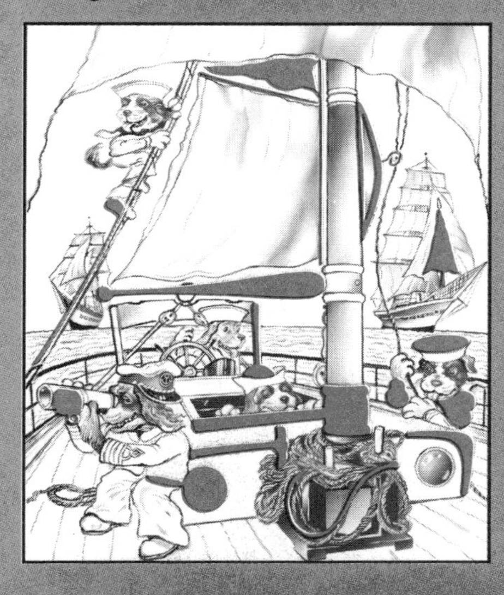

▼Pages 116-117

▼Page 118

▼Page 119

▼Page 120

Answers

▼Page 121

▼Pages 122–123

▼Page 124

▼Page 125

▼Page 126

▼Page 127

Published by Highlights for Children
P.O. Box 18201
Columbus, Ohio 43218-0201
Printed in the United States of America
ISBN: 978-1-62091-774-9

Second edition, 2017
Visit our website at Highlights.com.
10 9 8 7 6 5 4 3 2